THE JOURNEY OF THE SELF

AUTHOR MY SELF

RAGHU. JUPUDI

Made with ♥ on the Notion Press Platform
www.notionpress.com

To every soul who has ever felt lost, broken, or uncertain—
This book is for you.

To those standing at life's crossroads, unsure of which path to take, yet still willing to take a step forward.
To the ones who have fallen, and instead of giving up, chose to rise—stronger, wiser, and more resilient.
To the dreamers who refuse to settle, the seekers who crave meaning, and the silent warriors who fight invisible battles every day.

This book is dedicated to your courage.
To your decision to not remain stuck in your past.
To your willingness to rebuild your life from the ground up, with nothing but hope in your heart and fire in your spirit.

May these pages be a mirror to your potential, a map for your transformation, and a reminder that the journey to becoming your true self is the greatest journey you will ever take.

You are not alone.
And you are not done yet.

Keep going. Your future is waiting.

Contents

Foreword

We live in a world of noise—expectations, comparisons, endless scrolling, and voices that tell us who we should be. Somewhere along the way, many of us lose sight of who we truly are. We wear masks, chase goals that aren't ours, and silence the quiet voice within that keeps asking, "Is this all there is?"

This book is a response to that voice.

The Journey to the Self is not just a guide—it's a companion. A mirror. A spark. It was born from a desire to help young men—and anyone seeking clarity—rediscover their essence, reclaim their purpose, and build a life rooted in peace, meaning, and authenticity.

What you hold in your hands is more than just words. It's a conversation—a dialogue between a curious young seeker and a wise philosopher. In their exchange, you'll see reflections of your own questions, struggles, dreams, and fears. Through their journey, you'll uncover timeless truths, practical tools, and gentle reminders that the answers you seek are already within you.

This is not a book that gives you rules to live by. It gives you insight—so that you can create your own path, guided by awareness, discipline, and inner strength. It draws from ancient wisdom, modern psychology, and real-life experience, offering a framework for transformation that is both soulful and practical.

As you read, pause often. Reflect. Write. Feel. Let the words sink in. Allow the silence between the lines to speak to you.

Because this isn't just a book.

It's an invitation.

To return to yourself.
To rise.
To begin again.
Welcome to the journey.

Preface

There comes a moment in every life when the outer world no longer satisfies the questions burning within. A moment when achievement feels empty, routines feel meaningless, and the soul begins to whisper, "There's more to you than this."

I wrote this book in response to that whisper. Not just for you—but for the younger version of myself who once felt lost, restless, and disconnected from who he truly was. I've walked through the fog of confusion, battled the storms of doubt, and stood at the edge of giving up, wondering if change was even possible.

And yet, something within kept calling me forward. That call was not to escape life—but to meet it fully. To understand myself. To find clarity. To live with intention and courage.

The Journey to the Self is the path I discovered and continue to walk. It is a path of awareness, discipline, self-respect, and silent strength. Through the conversations in this book—between a young man and a wise philosopher—I've tried to capture the universal inner journey we all must take: the one that leads us inward before we can rise outward.

This book is divided into four parts—each one guiding you deeper into the foundation of a meaningful life:
Self-Awareness, to help you see clearly;
Discipline & Purpose, to help you build strength;
Inner Mastery, to help you rise above noise and fear;
and Leadership & Legacy, to help you lead with heart and live beyond yourself.

Each chapter offers stories, reflections, practical steps, and timeless truths drawn from life, philosophy, and the Bhagavad Gita. It's not about perfection—it's about progress. Not about being someone else—but becoming more of who you already are.

This book is for those who want to rebuild their life from the inside out. For those who believe that peace is power. That clarity is freedom. And that our greatest success is becoming our truest self.

Thank you for picking up this book. May it speak to your heart, awaken your spirit, and walk beside you as you step into the beautiful, bold journey that is waiting for you.

With strength and purpose,
Raghu. Jupudi

Acknowledgements

Writing this book has been one of the most soul-stirring journeys of my life. And like every great journey, it was not traveled alone.

First and foremost, I offer my deepest gratitude to the Divine force within and around me—the silent guide who kept showing the way when I doubted my own steps. This book exists because of that invisible presence and unwavering inner whisper: “Keep going.”

To my family—your love is my foundation. Your belief in me, even when unspoken, gave me the strength to write, reflect, and rise. Thank you for holding space for me through every season of life.

To my mentors, friends, and those rare souls who challenged me to think deeply, live truthfully, and walk with integrity—your words and presence have shaped me more than you’ll ever know.

To every young man who ever shared his struggles, dreams, or confusion with me—you are the reason this book was written. Your honesty inspired these pages. Your desire to grow moved me to write with clarity and compassion.

To the readers—thank you for choosing this book and trusting it to be part of your journey. I hope you find in it what I found in writing it: a reminder that you are not lost, you are simply becoming.

Lastly, to the younger me—the boy who once carried questions heavier than he knew how to answer—thank you for not giving up. This book is the letter you needed, and I hope it reaches everyone else who needs it too.

With love,
Raghu. Jupudi

Prologue

There are moments in life when everything we've known begins to feel unfamiliar. Moments when the world outside seems to lose its color, and we are left searching—lost between who we were and who we are meant to become.

Perhaps you are standing in one of those moments now. Perhaps you've been searching for answers, for meaning, or for a way to break free from the noise and confusion of everyday life. If so, you are not alone.

This book is not about giving you easy answers. It is not a collection of methods or shortcuts to success. Instead, it is an invitation—an invitation to embark on the greatest journey you will ever take: the journey to the self.

You might wonder, what is the "self"?

It is the quiet part within you that has always known the truth. It is the essence of who you really are, beyond your titles, roles, and expectations. It is the part of you that has remained untouched by the chaos of the world, waiting patiently to be recognized.

But the journey to the self is not always easy. It requires facing discomfort, breaking old habits, and stepping into the unknown. It demands that we challenge our beliefs, confront our fears, and choose to move forward even when the path ahead is unclear. It asks us to look inward—to peel back the layers of conditioning, doubt, and insecurity, until we find the courage to stand in the truth of who we are.

This journey is not a destination—it is a process. And in that process, you will discover that you are far more capable, resilient, and powerful than you ever imagined. You will realize that every struggle, every setback, and every challenge is not something to fear, but something to embrace, because it is part of the growth that shapes you.

As you read these pages, remember: You are not here by accident. The words you are about to read are not just mine—they are the voice of every seeker who has ever wondered about their purpose, their place in the world, and their true self.

This book is not about transforming you into someone you are not. It is about helping you become more of who you already are—whole, powerful, and at peace with yourself.

So, take a deep breath, open your heart, and step forward. Your journey begins now.

1

Introduction

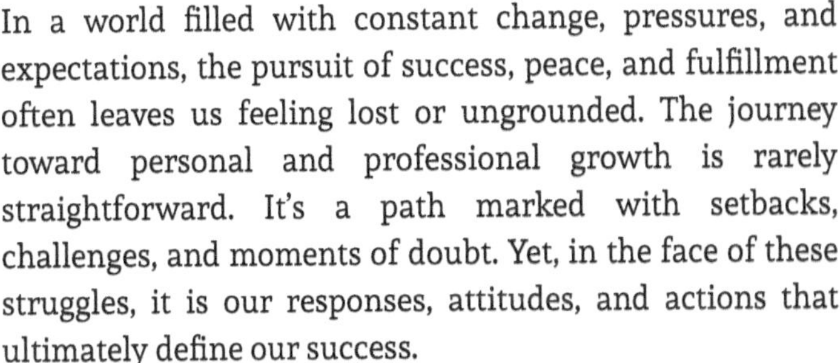

In a world filled with constant change, pressures, and expectations, the pursuit of success, peace, and fulfillment often leaves us feeling lost or ungrounded. The journey toward personal and professional growth is rarely straightforward. It's a path marked with setbacks, challenges, and moments of doubt. Yet, in the face of these struggles, it is our responses, attitudes, and actions that ultimately define our success.

This book is an exploration of how to live a meaningful life—a life where ambition, persistence, balance, and selflessness all coexist harmoniously. It isn't about avoiding failure or chasing perfection, but about embracing each step of the journey with purpose and clarity. By reflecting on the concepts of resilience, growth, and service to others, this book offers practical wisdom on how to approach life's challenges, find fulfillment in the present, and stay true to your goals.

Through an engaging dialogue between a philosopher and a young man, the lessons within these pages are designed to inspire you to examine your own beliefs, actions, and motivations. The ultimate purpose of this book is not to provide a formula for success, but rather to guide you on your path of continuous personal development, helping you realize that success lies not just in what you achieve, but in who you become in the process.

2

The Role of Purpose in Life

Introduction to Purpose

Purpose is the central driving force in human life. It gives us direction, meaning, and a sense of fulfillment. Without purpose, life can often feel aimless, and we may find ourselves adrift, lacking motivation or clarity. Purpose is the lens through which we perceive the world, make decisions, and take actions. But what truly defines our purpose, and how do we uncover it?

Many teachings from ancient wisdom to modern psychological frameworks offer profound perspectives on finding and living in alignment with one's purpose. These ideas, though varied, provide complementary wisdom that can guide individuals toward a more meaningful, intentional life.

Purpose in Wisdom Traditions

In various spiritual and philosophical traditions, the concept of purpose is intricately linked to fulfilling one's duty in life. One central teaching suggests that purpose is not about personal gain or the results of one's actions but rather about fulfilling one's duty and contributing to the greater good, without attachment to the outcome. The focus shifts from personal desires to aligning with a higher calling and responsibilities toward others and society.

This approach emphasizes that we should not be solely concerned with what we achieve or the outcomes we seek, but instead, we should focus on our duty and service to others. When we focus on what is our responsibility in the greater order of things, purpose becomes clearer and more fulfilling.

Discovering Your Purpose: Passion, Strengths, and Service

Purpose is not just about personal achievement; it is also about finding ways to contribute to the world. One way to understand purpose is through the intersection of what you love, what you are good at, what the world needs, and what you can sustain over time. When these elements align, life feels purposeful.

The true essence of purpose lies in discovering what brings joy, what you excel at, and how these can be directed toward the needs of others. This process of self-discovery is essential for creating a life that feels aligned with who we truly are, both personally and in relation to the world around us.

Building Purpose through Small Actions

Purpose doesn't have to be a distant, overwhelming concept. In fact, the best way to uncover and live out your purpose is through small, consistent actions. When you begin to take deliberate steps each day that reflect your values, you are actively shaping a life aligned with your larger goals.

It is not about setting grand, far-off aspirations alone, but rather about creating systems and habits that align with who you want to be. Small, incremental actions build up over time, contributing to a much larger transformation. Consistent efforts, no matter how minor they seem, have the power to shape your identity and connect you with your purpose.

Living Authentically: The Courage to Choose Your Path

Living in alignment with your true purpose requires the courage to live authentically, free from the pressure of external validation. Too often, people get caught up in seeking approval from others, trying to meet societal expectations, or chasing after an idealized version of success. However, the real challenge of life is to free yourself from these external influences and live according to your true self.

Living authentically means making choices based on your values and desires, not what others think or expect of you. When you live true to who you are, you begin to align your actions with your purpose, and fulfillment follows. It is through this courage to be yourself that you unlock your greatest potential.

Bringing It All Together

The pursuit of purpose is a deeply personal journey that involves understanding who we are, what we value, and how we can contribute to the world. By integrating wisdom from various teachings and philosophies, we begin to see purpose not as a distant goal but as a guiding principle that shapes our thoughts, actions, and relationships.

- Purpose is about fulfilling one's duties and responsibilities, in alignment with a higher order.
- True fulfillment arises when we find the intersection of our passions, strengths, and the needs of the world.
- Our daily habits and systems play a crucial role in aligning our actions with our larger purpose.

- The courage to live authentically and true to our own values is essential for uncovering and fulfilling our purpose.

When we integrate these teachings into our lives, we begin to live a life of clarity and intention. The journey toward purpose is not linear; it is a process of discovery, growth, and continual refinement.

Practical Steps to Discovering Your Purpose

- **Reflect on Your Values**: Take time to identify what truly matters to you. What values do you hold dear? These will serve as the foundation for your purpose.
- **Explore Your Passions and Talents**: What activities bring you joy? What are you naturally good at? Your passions and strengths are key elements of your purpose.
- **Understand the Needs of the World**: How can your unique skills and talents serve others? Purpose is often found in contributing to the greater good.
- **Set Identity-Based Goals**: Focus on becoming the person you want to be, not just on what you want to achieve.
- **Let Go of External Validation**: Your purpose should be about living authentically, not about meeting others' expectations.

3

Transforming Habits for Lasting Change

Introduction to Habits and Change

Habits are the invisible forces that shape our daily lives. They dictate much of what we do, how we think, and how we react to situations. While we often believe that change requires large, sweeping actions, the truth is that lasting transformation comes from small, consistent habits. These tiny actions, repeated over time, build the foundation for major shifts in our lives.

The process of change can seem daunting, but when we understand how habits work and how they influence our behavior, we can leverage them to create the life we desire. By transforming our habits, we transform ourselves. But how do we cultivate good habits and break free from those that no longer serve us?

The Power of Small Changes

The key to lasting change lies in making small, incremental improvements rather than attempting dramatic overhauls. One of the most effective ways to build lasting habits is by focusing on the system, not just the goal.

Goals are important, but systems—the routines and habits we follow—are what make success inevitable.

Consider how tiny adjustments, compounded over time, lead to significant results. A single push-up today won't transform your body, but 100 push-ups each day for a year will make a noticeable difference. It's not about making huge leaps; it's about making small, consistent efforts that build momentum. This approach allows for sustainable growth, rather than the burnout often associated with attempting to make dramatic changes all at once.

Building Habits That Align with Your Purpose

When we talk about habits, it's essential to understand that they must align with our deeper purpose and values. Simply adopting habits without reflecting on their purpose can lead to superficial results. For habits to truly be effective, they must connect with the larger vision of who we want to become.

Start by asking yourself: What kind of person do I want to be? Instead of focusing solely on outcomes—such as getting fit or being more productive—shift the focus to the type of identity you wish to cultivate. For example, rather than setting a goal to run a marathon, aim to become a person who values physical activity and health. In doing so, your habits will naturally align with your deeper purpose and become a reflection of the person you are striving to be.

The Science of Habit Formation

Habits are created through a process of cue, craving, response, and reward. First, there is a trigger, or cue, that sets off the habit loop. This could be an internal feeling or an external event. Next, there is a craving—an emotional or psychological desire that motivates us to act. This craving prompts a response, which is the habit itself. Finally, the reward reinforces the habit, making it more likely that we'll repeat the behavior.

Understanding this cycle gives us the power to manipulate it. By making the cue for a positive habit obvious and the reward satisfying, we can condition ourselves to repeat the behavior. On the other hand, we can break bad habits by disrupting one of these stages—either by removing the cue, replacing the craving, or changing the reward system.

Creating a Habit-Positive Environment

One of the easiest ways to build better habits is to create an environment that supports them. Our surroundings influence our behavior more than we realize. For instance, if you want to eat healthier, keep nutritious foods visible and accessible, and place unhealthy snacks out of sight. If you aim to be more productive, ensure your workspace is organized and free from distractions.

The key is to make the right behaviors easier and the wrong behaviors harder. This environmental design principle helps to reinforce the habits you want to build by eliminating friction. The less effort it takes to engage in positive habits, the more likely they are to stick.

Breaking Bad Habits

Breaking bad habits requires a deeper understanding of the underlying triggers and motivations. It's not enough to simply say, "I want to stop smoking" or "I want to stop procrastinating." Instead, identify the cue that triggers the unwanted behavior, the craving that drives it, and the reward that reinforces it.

Once you pinpoint these factors, you can work backward to disrupt the habit loop. For example, if procrastination is triggered by feeling overwhelmed with a task, break the task into smaller, manageable steps to reduce the feeling of being overwhelmed. If you're trying to quit a bad habit like overeating, replace the craving for comfort food with a healthier alternative, like going for a walk or practicing deep breathing.

The process of breaking a bad habit is not about simply eliminating it but replacing it with a new, more constructive behavior. Over time, the new habit will take the place of the old one, creating a positive feedback loop.

The Role of Patience and Consistency

When transforming habits, patience and consistency are key. The process of habit formation takes time, and results are often not immediate. The tendency to want quick results can undermine the process, leading to frustration and discouragement. It's important to remember that habits are cumulative; the effects are often delayed, but over time, they compound and lead to significant change.

Consistency doesn't mean perfection. There will be times when you slip up or fall short, but the key is to not let these setbacks derail your progress. The more consistently you practice your habits, the more they will become ingrained in your daily life. Even small failures are part of the process, as they provide opportunities for learning and growth.

Creating a Sustainable Habit System

To truly transform your life, you must build a system of habits that align with your goals and purpose. It's not about a one-time effort but about creating a sustainable system that becomes part of who you are. This system should be flexible enough to adapt to changes in your life but structured enough to keep you on track.

The process of building lasting change involves reflection, experimentation, and iteration. It's about making incremental improvements over time and focusing on continuous growth. As your system of habits evolves, you'll find that your life becomes more purposeful and intentional.

Bringing It All Together

Creating lasting change through habit transformation is not about a sudden, dramatic shift but about the steady accumulation of small, purposeful actions. By focusing on building habits that align with your deeper purpose, you can create a system that supports your growth and leads to meaningful, lasting transformation.

- Focus on small, incremental changes that compound over time.
- Build habits that align with your values and identity, not just your goals.
- Understand the habit loop—cue, craving, response, reward—and use it to your advantage.
- Design your environment to make positive habits easier and negative ones harder.
- Break bad habits by disrupting the habit loop and replacing them with healthier behaviors.
- Be patient and consistent, knowing that real change takes time.

By embracing the power of small, consistent habits, you can create lasting change in your life. The process may not always be easy, but it is always worth it.

Transforming Habits for Lasting Change

The Young Man:
(Leaning forward, eager)
I've been thinking a lot about habits lately, but it feels like the more I try, the harder it gets to make real change. I understand change is necessary, but how can I really make it stick?

The Philosopher:
(Smiling gently, with a calm tone)
Ah, change... The most profound aspect of our existence. It is not in grand gestures that change occurs, my young friend, but in the small, almost invisible choices we make every day. Habits, you see, are the silent architects of our lives. They sculpt who we are, who we become. What you are today is the product of the habits you've practiced—consciously or unconsciously—for years.

The Young Man:
(Confused, fidgeting slightly)
So, you're saying that change doesn't have to be some grand leap, right? It's more about the things I do every day? But... I still don't get it. What makes habits so powerful?

The Philosopher:
(Tilting head thoughtfully)
Imagine the river. A single drop of water doesn't seem to

carry much power, does it? But when that drop joins millions of others, day by day, year after year, it carves valleys, shapes mountains, and even creates new landscapes. Habits are the drops of water, my young friend. At first, they seem trivial. One small action doesn't change much. But as they accumulate over time, they begin to transform the very core of your being.

The Young Man:
(Nods, but still unsure)
I think I understand... but then why do I struggle with consistency? I try to adopt new habits, but I can never keep them up for long. What's the secret to making them stick?

The Philosopher:
(Pauses, looking contemplative)
Ah, the challenge of consistency. It is not the fault of the habit, but of the system you create around it. You see, we often focus too much on the goal—the distant mountain we wish to climb—without considering the daily steps needed to reach the summit. The journey is in the routine, not the end destination.

The key is in understanding who you wish to become. Your habits must reflect that identity. If you want to be someone who values health, for example, don't make it about working out to lose weight. No, make it about being the kind of person who cherishes the gift of life and energy. When you identify as that person, the actions that support that identity will flow more naturally.

The Young Man:

(Squinting, thinking deeply)

So... instead of focusing on just the goal—like losing weight or getting stronger—I should think of myself as someone who is healthy, and then build habits that match that? That's a shift in thinking. But how do I start? Where do I even begin?

The Philosopher:

(Gently smiles)

The beginning is always where we find ourselves, no matter how far we've traveled. Start small. Small actions lead to bigger transformations. The process is gradual. Begin with something simple—something that feels doable. Don't ask for miracles, but for consistency in the simplest of practices. Perhaps, drink a glass of water every morning. Take a ten-minute walk. These are small, yes, but with time, they shape the future you. The key is that you must start, and start with something that connects with the person you are becoming.

The Young Man:

(Slowly nodding, absorbing the wisdom)

I get it now. It's not about grand gestures—it's about small actions that align with who I am becoming. But... how do I understand the real mechanism behind habits? Why do some stick and others don't?

The Philosopher:

(Pauses, with a knowing look)

Ah, the mechanics of habits... Let me tell you a secret: all habits are driven by a cycle. A cycle of cue, craving, response, and reward. The cue is the trigger—something that tells your mind, "It's time to act." Then comes the craving, the desire that rises within you, urging you to respond. The response is the habit itself, the action you take. And finally, the reward—this is what solidifies the loop. It reinforces the action, creating the desire to repeat it.

The Young Man:
(Perking up)
So, it's like a loop that gets stronger each time it's repeated, right? But... how do I build a new habit? How do I get the reward to match my effort?

The Philosopher:
(Leaning forward, with a soft smile)
Yes, the loop is powerful. To build a new habit, you must first make the cue clear and visible. Let it call to you, reminding you that it is time to act. Then, the craving must be something that deeply resonates with you. The more meaningful the craving, the more powerful the action will be. After the response, make sure the reward is immediate and satisfying. It doesn't have to be grand—it could be something as simple as a feeling of accomplishment, or a moment of joy in completing the task.

The Young Man:
(Tilting head, clearly thinking)
So, if I want to develop a habit of running, I could start by

laying out my shoes the night before—making it easy for me to see them in the morning. The craving could be the energy I feel after the run, and the reward could be that sense of achievement, or perhaps a good breakfast afterward. Right?

The Philosopher:

(With a smile of approval)

Exactly. Now, think of your bad habits. They too follow this same cycle, but perhaps you've not been conscious of it. If you want to break a bad habit, you must identify the cue, the craving, the response, and the reward—and then disrupt it. Change one link in the chain. Let's say you're trying to break the habit of snacking late at night. Identify the cue—perhaps it's stress, boredom, or the desire to feel comforted. Then, replace the craving with something healthier, like deep breathing, reading, or a warm cup of tea. When you disrupt the cycle, the bad habit begins to lose its power.

The Young Man:

(Reflecting deeply)

I see now. It's not just about stopping the bad habit, but replacing it with something better, something that satisfies me in a more positive way. But, philosopher, what if I fail? What if I can't keep it up?

The Philosopher:

(Laughs softly, looking wise)

Ah, failure... It is not to be feared, my young friend. Failure is the soil from which growth springs. Perfection is an illusion. Consistency, however, is real. If you fall, rise again. A setback is merely a lesson—a chance to reflect, adapt, and try anew. The secret to growth lies not in avoiding failure, but in embracing it with humility, and in using it to refine your path.

The Young Man:
(Nods with a newfound understanding, a smile forming)
That's very comforting to hear. It's not about perfection—it's about progress. Little steps, every day, right?

The Philosopher:
(With a serene smile)
Yes, little steps. And those steps will lead you to a life that reflects your deepest values. Habits, when practiced with intention, will reshape you into the person you truly wish to become. But remember, it is not the mountain that you climb, but the journey itself. Be patient with the process. The river does not rush to carve the valley, but it does so steadily.

The Young Man:
(Smiling, more at ease)
I think I understand now. Thank you for the guidance. I'll start small, and focus on consistency. The rest will follow.

4

The Power of Purpose and Meaning

The Young Man:
(Sitting quietly, clearly contemplating)
I've been thinking about something for a while now. I see people who are successful, who seem so sure of what they're doing and where they're going. But I feel... lost sometimes. How do I even begin to find my purpose?

The Philosopher:
(Laughs softly, looking at him with understanding)
Ah, the search for purpose. A journey that many of us undertake, yet few truly understand. Purpose is not something you *find* as much as something you *create*—in your actions, your thoughts, and the choices you make each day. It is the thread that ties your existence to something greater, something beyond mere survival.

The Young Man:
(Pause, leaning forward)
So, purpose isn't something that just comes to us in a moment of clarity? I always thought that one day, it would just *hit* me, you know?

The Philosopher:
(Shakes head with a gentle smile)
No, it is not a sudden, grand revelation. It is found in the everyday moments, the small decisions, and the values you hold dear. Purpose is shaped by the way you live your life—by how you approach others, how you approach challenges, and most importantly, how you respond to the world around you. It is in *doing* that we discover the deeper meaning of *being*.

The Young Man:
(Nods slowly, still not entirely clear)
But how do I know if I'm on the right path? How do I even start living with purpose?

The Philosopher:
(Thoughtfully)
Begin by asking yourself what matters most to you. Look beyond the superficial desires—the things society tells you to chase—and dig deeper. What stirs your soul? What gives you a sense of fulfillment beyond fleeting satisfaction? Your purpose is hidden in the things that make you feel alive, the things that resonate with your core. It's often a combination of what you love, what you're good at, and what the world needs.

The Young Man:
(Looks curious)
So, purpose is like a blend of passion, skill, and service? That makes sense. But sometimes, I feel like my passion is too scattered. How do I narrow it down?

The Philosopher:
(Smiling wisely)
You do not need to narrow your passion immediately. Passion evolves, and in time, it will lead you to your unique purpose. Start with what excites you now, and let it unfold.

Even if your passions seem scattered, the act of pursuing them will bring clarity. It is only when you try to express your deepest desires in the world that you begin to see how they fit together.

The Young Man:

(Reflecting on this)

So, I should just start somewhere—even if it feels a little unclear? I shouldn't wait for the perfect moment or perfect clarity?

The Philosopher:

(With quiet conviction)

Yes. Waiting for perfection only leads to stagnation. Purpose reveals itself through action. The smallest step you take towards what you feel drawn to will lead you toward greater understanding. It's in the doing, not the waiting, that you find your true direction.

The Young Man:

(Leans back, looking a little relieved)

That sounds less overwhelming. But what if I make the wrong choice? What if I go down a path that doesn't align with my true purpose?

The Philosopher:

(Gently, with a knowing tone)

Ah, my young friend, there is no "wrong" choice when you are seeking with intention. Even if the path you walk leads to an obstacle, that too becomes part of the journey. Purpose is not about finding one right answer; it is about constantly learning, adapting, and evolving. The key is not to be afraid of mistakes. Each misstep teaches you more about what matters and brings you closer to your true calling.

The Young Man:

(Sighs, looking thoughtful)

So, the fear of failure shouldn't hold me back from pursuing what I want to do? It's okay to try and fail?

The Philosopher:

(Pauses, looking deeply into his eyes)

Fear is a natural companion on the journey of purpose. It will always be with you, whispering doubts and urging you to stay comfortable. But, my friend, it is not the absence of fear that leads to greatness—it is the ability to move forward despite it. Failure is not an enemy; it is the greatest teacher you will ever have. Through failure, you sharpen your understanding, adjust your course, and grow stronger.

The Young Man:

(Nods, starting to feel more empowered)

That makes sense. Failure is just part of the process. But how does all of this connect to the way we live our daily lives? I mean, how does purpose play into the small, mundane tasks?

The Philosopher:

(With a quiet smile)

Ah, the mundane. It is in the smallest of tasks that purpose is often revealed. You see, purpose is not something that exists only in grand gestures or future accomplishments. It is in the way you fold your clothes, how you greet the cashier at the store, the care you put into each action, no matter how small. When you approach each task with intention and mindfulness, it becomes an expression of your deeper values and your sense of purpose.

The Young Man:

(Laughing a little)

So, even the little things matter? I guess I never really thought of it that way. But what about when things get hard? When life feels overwhelming and uncertain?

The Philosopher:

(Looking wise and steady)

Ah, those are the moments when purpose is tested. Life's challenges are inevitable. They are the storms that come to clear the path. It is in these moments that you must remind yourself of why you began. Keep your eyes on the vision that brought you here. When you encounter resistance, see it not as a barrier, but as an opportunity to grow, to strengthen your resolve. Purpose doesn't vanish in hard times; it deepens.

The Young Man:

(With newfound clarity)

I think I understand now. Purpose isn't a destination—it's in the way we live each day, in every small action. And when life gets hard, it's not a reason to give up, but an opportunity to grow stronger.

The Philosopher:

(Softly, with a final piece of wisdom)

Exactly. Remember, purpose is not a place to arrive at—it is a way of being. When you live with purpose, every moment is imbued with meaning. Every step, every action, becomes a reflection of your inner values. And when that happens, my young friend, you will walk through life with a quiet strength, a deep sense of peace.

The Young Man:

(Smiling, feeling a sense of peace)

I'm beginning to see it now. It's about creating purpose through every action, every choice. It's not about waiting for the perfect moment. I just need to start.

5

The Role of Discipline and Willpower

The Young Man:
(Sitting quietly, appearing deep in thought)
I've been thinking a lot about willpower. Sometimes, I can be so motivated to change, but after a few days, I lose momentum. Why does it feel so hard to keep going, even when I know I need to?

The Philosopher:
(Laughs softly, as though anticipating the question)
Ah, the challenge of willpower. It is an energy, like a flame that burns bright at first but can easily flicker out if not fed properly. Willpower is not something we have in unlimited supply. It's like a muscle—at first, it's strong, but if overused without rest or replenishment, it becomes fatigued. The key is not in trying to force it constantly but in nurturing it.

The Young Man:
(Leaning in, intrigued)
So, it's not about pushing harder? What do you mean by nurturing it?

The Philosopher:
(Thoughtfully)
Discipline is what sustains willpower. Without discipline, willpower is like a flickering candle, burning bright one moment and out the next. To nurture willpower, you must first create structures, routines, and habits that require minimal decision-making. In this way, you conserve your energy for the moments when you really need it. The more you rely on habit, the less you need to depend on willpower to get things done.

The Young Man:
(Nods, thinking)
That makes sense. So, it's not about forcing myself to always stay strong. It's about making things automatic through discipline. But what happens when life throws unexpected challenges my way? How do I stay disciplined then?

The Philosopher:
(Smiling gently)
Life will always throw challenges at you. It is not a matter of avoiding them but of how you respond to them. When discipline becomes a way of life, it doesn't break at the first sign of resistance. Instead, it becomes flexible, adaptable. If your goal is to meditate every day, for instance, but one day you're too tired, discipline doesn't mean pushing through at all costs. It means adjusting the goal—perhaps meditating for just five minutes instead of twenty. The key is to remain consistent, not rigid.

The Young Man:
(Sighing, relieved)
So, it's okay to adjust? I used to think that if I didn't follow through perfectly, I was failing.

The Philosopher:
(With a knowing look)

Ah, the perfection trap. It is a powerful illusion. Discipline is not about perfection, but about consistency and intention. It's about showing up for yourself, even when you're not at your best. Perfectionism creates unnecessary pressure. Flexibility, however, allows you to keep moving forward, no matter the circumstances.

The Young Man:

(Nods thoughtfully)

I think I understand now. It's not about being perfect; it's about being consistent and flexible. But how do I make sure I don't burn out? How do I avoid overloading myself with too many commitments?

The Philosopher:

(Taking a slow breath, as though considering the question carefully)

That, my friend, is a crucial question. Discipline is about balance. It's not about pushing yourself beyond your limits but about knowing your limits and respecting them. When you stretch yourself too thin, you drain your willpower and energy. Prioritize your goals, and learn to say no to things that don't align with your true purpose. The more focused your efforts, the more sustainable your discipline will be.

The Young Man:

(Smiling, a weight lifting off his shoulders)

It sounds like discipline isn't about doing everything at once. It's about doing the right things, and doing them regularly, without overwhelming myself.

The Philosopher:

(Smiling in return)

Precisely. Discipline is a marathon, not a sprint. It's the steady, consistent efforts over time that yield the greatest rewards.

6

The Art of Mindfulness and Presence

The Young Man:

(Watching the sun set, contemplative)

I've been hearing a lot about mindfulness lately. People keep saying I should be more present, but I have no idea how to actually do that. What does being present even mean?

The Philosopher:

(Looking at the horizon, smiling softly)

Ah, presence. It is the art of being fully here, in the now, without being lost in thought about the past or the future. Most people live their lives either reliving old memories or imagining future scenarios. The present moment, however, is the only place where life truly exists. The key is to learn how to tune in, to engage fully with whatever is in front of you, without distraction.

The Young Man:

(Looks confused, still struggling)

But how do I do that? My mind is always racing, thinking about what I should do next, or what happened earlier. How do I stay in the moment?

The Philosopher:

(Pauses, choosing his words carefully)

Start by focusing on your senses. Notice the sound of your breath, the feeling of your feet on the ground, the warmth of the sun on your skin. When you pay attention to your senses, your mind can't wander as easily. It grounds you in the here and now.

Mindfulness is about bringing your awareness to the present moment without judgment. When your mind starts to wander, gently bring it back to the task at hand, whether it's drinking a cup of tea or having a conversation. Be fully present in whatever you are doing, without rushing or expecting anything from it.

The Young Man:

(Considering the idea)

So, it's really about noticing the small things, like the feel of my breath or the sensation in my body? It's not about stopping thoughts, but about not letting them take over?

The Philosopher:

(Nods approvingly)

Exactly. Mindfulness isn't about suppressing your thoughts; it's about observing them without attachment. You are not your thoughts. They come and go like clouds in the sky. But the sky remains. You are the sky—the awareness, the stillness. When you recognize this, you begin to live in the present moment with a deep sense of peace.

The Young Man:

(Smiling as the realization dawns)

It's like stepping back from my thoughts, just observing them without getting caught up. I think I've been living too much in my head. But how do I keep this up when life gets busy?

The Philosopher:

(Thoughtfully)

Life will always be busy, my friend. The challenge is not to wait for calm, but to find calm amidst the chaos. You don't need hours of quiet to be mindful. You can practice mindfulness in the small moments—when you're waiting in line, washing dishes, or walking to work. These moments are opportunities to return to the present, to practice being here now. It is in these moments that you cultivate the habit of mindfulness.

The Young Man:

(Smiling, feeling more relaxed)

I think I'm starting to get it. It's not about carving out extra time; it's about bringing my awareness to whatever I'm already doing.

The Philosopher:

(Smiling gently)

Yes. And when you can live in the present, your life begins to shift. You experience more joy, more clarity, and more peace. You stop chasing after happiness and begin to realize that it is already here, in this very moment.

7

The Power of Resilience and Adversity

The Young Man:

(Looking troubled, his voice filled with frustration)

I've been trying so hard to make progress, but no matter what I do, life keeps throwing obstacles in my way. It's like every time I take a step forward, something sets me back. How do I keep going when it feels like everything is against me?

The Philosopher:

(Looking at him with calm, understanding eyes)

Ah, the weight of adversity. It is something everyone faces, yet it can feel uniquely personal when you're in the middle of it. But, my young friend, what you are experiencing is not failure. It is the forge that shapes you. The difficulties you face are not meant to break you but to build you, to test your resilience and determination.

The Young Man:

(Sighing deeply)

It's hard to see how setbacks could possibly be good for me. I just want things to go smoothly for once.

The Philosopher:

(With a small smile)

That is a common desire—wanting smooth sailing, wanting the journey to be without bumps. But you see, it is in the struggle, the overcoming of obstacles, that true growth happens. Resilience is built in those very moments when life feels the hardest. It is the capacity to rise again, not after the first fall, but after the hundredth.

The Young Man:

(Frowning, trying to understand)

But how do I keep getting back up when it feels like nothing is working? I feel like I'm not making any real progress.

The Philosopher:

(Leaning in, speaking with a deep wisdom)

Resilience is not about never falling—it's about never allowing a fall to define you. It is about seeing setbacks as temporary and learning from each one. You do not rise because everything goes right. You rise because you choose to stand again, even when the odds are stacked against you. Each time you rise, you become stronger, more capable.

The Young Man:

(Pause, thinking deeply)

So, resilience isn't about avoiding failure—it's about how we respond to it?

The Philosopher:

(With a nod)

Exactly. Resilience is forged in your response to adversity. It is the decision to persist in the face of challenges. It is the understanding that no matter how many times you are knocked down, you have the power to rise again. Every time you stand up, you add another layer to your strength, another stone to the foundation of your character.

The Young Man:
(Quietly, looking thoughtful)
But sometimes, I wonder if I'm strong enough to keep going. I feel like I don't have what it takes. How do I know if I can endure what's ahead?

The Philosopher:
(Putting a hand on his shoulder, looking him in the eyes)
Ah, the doubt. It is natural. The moment you question your strength, you are already on the path to discovering it. It is through the very doubts you carry that you uncover the depth of your resilience. The seed of strength lies within you, but it only grows when you face adversity and choose not to give in. You have far more strength than you realize. When life seems darkest, that is when your light shines brightest.

The Young Man:
(Slowly nodding, a sense of realization dawning)
I see. It's not about having the strength before the challenge—it's about finding it in the middle of the challenge. So, I have to trust that I'm capable, even when it feels impossible?

The Philosopher:
(Smiling gently)
Yes. Resilience is not a quality you are born with; it is something you cultivate through your actions and your choices. The more you trust in your own capacity to overcome, the more resilient you become. And remember, you are never alone in your struggle. Others have faced similar battles, and many have come out stronger on the other side. You are part of a long, unbroken lineage of human strength.

The Young Man:
(Looking more at ease)

That's comforting to hear. It's not about being perfect or having everything figured out right away. It's about learning to stand again, even when things get tough.

The Philosopher:

(With a soft smile)

Exactly. And remember, the toughest storms often bring the clearest skies. You may not see the benefit of the challenge in the moment, but in hindsight, you will see how each difficulty helped shape you into the person you are meant to become. Through adversity, you will learn who you truly are and what you are capable of.

The Young Man:

(With a determined expression)

I'm starting to feel a shift. Maybe setbacks aren't as bad as I thought. Maybe they're exactly what I need to grow stronger.

The Philosopher:

(Grinning)

Indeed. Life's greatest lessons often come wrapped in difficulty. Embrace them, my young friend, for they are the ones that will teach you the most.

8

The Importance of Self-Awareness

The Young Man:
(Sitting in a quiet corner, looking contemplative)
I've been thinking about something. I hear people say that knowing yourself is the key to everything. But what does that even mean? How do I really know who I am?

The Philosopher:
(With a thoughtful gaze)
Ah, self-awareness. It is the foundation of all growth. To know yourself is not just to understand your likes and dislikes, your strengths and weaknesses. It is to understand your thoughts, your emotions, and the patterns that govern your actions. It is the ability to step back and observe yourself without judgment, without attachment. When you truly know yourself, you gain the power to make choices that align with your deepest values.

The Young Man:
(Looking confused)
So, knowing yourself isn't just about what you like to do or what you're good at? It's more than that?

The Philosopher:
(Nods)
Yes. Self-awareness goes deeper. It involves understanding the forces that shape you—the beliefs you hold, the habits you've formed, the stories you tell yourself about who you are. It is about becoming aware of the ways in which you react to the world, rather than merely responding unconsciously. When you understand yourself at this level, you can begin to make conscious choices that reflect your true nature.

The Young Man:
(Thoughtfully)
But how do I uncover all of that? I feel like I'm always too busy to really think about who I am. Is there a way to start?

The Philosopher:
(Smiling)
The process of self-awareness begins with stillness. Take time to reflect—whether through meditation, journaling, or simply sitting quietly with your thoughts. Ask yourself deep questions: Why do I react the way I do? What are my deepest fears? What motivates me? The more you ask yourself these questions, the more you will begin to understand the patterns that shape your behavior. You will begin to see your true self, beyond the surface level.

The Young Man:
(Nods slowly)
I see. It's about creating space to reflect and truly listen to myself, rather than just running through life without thinking about my actions.

The Philosopher:
(With a gentle smile)
Exactly. And as you grow in self-awareness, you'll begin to make decisions from a place of clarity, not confusion. You

will be able to identify the things that align with your true values and let go of the things that don't. It's the beginning of living with intention.

The Young Man:

(Feeling more enlightened)

I'm starting to see how important this is. When I understand myself, I can choose my path more consciously. It's like being the author of my own story.

The Philosopher:

(Smiling warmly)

That's right. Self-awareness is the compass that guides you on your journey. It is the key to living authentically, to making decisions that lead you to a life of purpose and fulfillment. When you truly know yourself, the world becomes clearer, and the path ahead becomes easier to navigate.

9

The Importance of Patience and Long-Term Vision

The Young Man:
(Looking frustrated, tapping his fingers impatiently)
I feel like I'm stuck. I've been working hard, but it doesn't seem like I'm getting anywhere fast. Why does everything take so long? I want results now, but it feels like I'm not making much progress.

The Philosopher:
(Laughing gently)
Ah, the impatience of youth. It's a powerful force, one that drives us to act quickly, to seek immediate gratification. But my young friend, progress is not always measured in how fast we move, but in the direction we move. True growth takes time, and the most meaningful accomplishments are often the ones that require patience.

The Young Man:
(Looking frustrated)

But how can I stay patient when it feels like I'm putting in all this effort and not seeing results? It's discouraging.

The Philosopher:
(Nods understandingly)
I know it can be hard. But consider this: a seed doesn't grow into a tree overnight. It requires time, nurturing, and care. You can't rush the process of growth. Patience doesn't mean passivity. It means trusting the process and understanding that everything unfolds in its own time.

The Young Man:
(Thinking carefully)
So, you're saying I should focus more on the process and less on immediate results? But how do I keep motivated when things aren't happening as quickly as I'd like?

The Philosopher:
(Smiling gently)
Motivation is fleeting. It comes and goes, and it can't be relied upon alone. But when you focus on the long-term vision, when you have a clear sense of purpose and direction, you will find the strength to keep going even when motivation fades. The key is to stay committed to your vision, even in the face of slow progress. It is not about how fast you go, but about how steady and consistent you are.

The Young Man:
(Looking skeptical)
But what if I'm not seeing any tangible progress after a long time? How do I know that what I'm doing is worth it?

The Philosopher:
(With a knowing smile)
Ah, that is the essence of true patience. When you trust in your vision and your purpose, the results will come in due time, but they may not always look like what you expect.

Sometimes, the growth happens in ways that are not immediately visible. It could be that you are building character, resilience, or gaining wisdom along the way. Progress is not always linear—it often comes in bursts, in moments of clarity and breakthrough, when you least expect it.

The Young Man:

(Nods slowly, trying to absorb this idea)

I see. So, even though I can't always see the results, I have to trust that they're happening in ways I might not be aware of?

The Philosopher:

(Smiling warmly)

Exactly. And remember, patience is not just about waiting; it's about how you wait. It's about being fully present in the moment, continuing to move forward with purpose, even when you can't see the immediate fruits of your labor. It is in those moments of quiet persistence that the most meaningful results emerge.

The Young Man:

(Sighing, but with a sense of relief)

That makes sense. I've been so focused on the end result that I forgot to appreciate the journey. I guess I need to find joy in the process, even if the results aren't obvious right away.

The Philosopher:

(Nods thoughtfully)

Indeed. The journey is where the growth happens. The more you embrace the process, the more patient you become with it. You begin to understand that success is not a destination but a continuous unfolding. And when you look back after years of steady effort, you will see just how far you've come—how much you've grown—often in ways you never imagined.

The Young Man:

(Smiling, feeling a sense of peace)

I think I'm starting to get it. It's not about rushing or obsessing over the end goal. It's about staying true to the vision and trusting the process, no matter how long it takes.

The Philosopher:

(Smiling warmly)

Exactly. And remember, even the slowest progress is still progress. A river does not rush to the ocean, yet over time it wears away mountains. Keep moving, keep growing, and trust that everything you are doing is contributing to the bigger picture.

The Young Man:

(Looking calm and more confident)

I'll try to remember that. I'm starting to feel more at peace with the idea of patience.

The Philosopher:

(With a final, reassuring smile)

Patience, my friend, is not just a virtue—it is the foundation of all lasting success. Trust the journey, and in time, you will see the results unfold in ways you couldn't have anticipated.

10

The Power of Gratitude and Acceptance

The Young Man:
(Sitting on a bench, staring at the ground, looking dejected)
I've been feeling frustrated lately. No matter how hard I try, things just don't seem to go my way. I can't help but feel resentful of everything that hasn't worked out for me.

The Philosopher:
(Looking at him with a gentle, understanding gaze)
I see. The weight of frustration and resentment is a heavy burden to carry. But tell me, my young friend, have you ever paused to consider all the things you have, rather than focusing solely on what you don't have?

The Young Man:
(Looking up, confused)
What do you mean? I can't seem to get what I want, and I feel stuck. How could focusing on what I have change anything?

The Philosopher:
(Smiling thoughtfully)
Gratitude is the key to shifting your perspective. It's about

learning to appreciate what you have, rather than focusing on what you lack. When you cultivate gratitude, it changes how you see the world. It allows you to accept what is, rather than constantly wishing for what isn't. This shift in mindset can bring a sense of peace and contentment, even in difficult times.

The Young Man:

(Still unsure)

But how can I be grateful when things aren't going the way I want them to? How do I accept things when I feel like I deserve more?

The Philosopher:

(With a gentle smile)

Acceptance is not about resigning yourself to a life of complacency. It is about recognizing that, in this moment, things are exactly as they need to be. By accepting what is, you free yourself from the resistance that causes suffering. And through gratitude, you begin to see the blessings that are already present, even in the most difficult situations.

The Young Man:

(Starting to understand)

So, acceptance isn't about giving up—it's about making peace with what is. And gratitude helps me see the positive in even the hardest moments?

The Philosopher:

(Nods)

Yes. When you practice gratitude, you train your mind to focus on the good in your life, rather than dwelling on the negative. It's a simple but powerful shift in perspective. And when you accept things as they are, you release the tension that comes from wishing for something different. This acceptance doesn't mean you stop striving for your goals—it simply means that you can pursue them with a heart full of peace, rather than frustration.

The Young Man:

(Smiling, a weight lifting off his shoulders)

I think I understand now. Gratitude helps me see what's already good in my life, and acceptance frees me from feeling frustrated with what I can't control.

The Philosopher:

(Smiling warmly)

Exactly. And when you live with gratitude and acceptance, you open yourself to a life of peace and fulfillment. The more you cultivate these qualities, the more you'll find that the world begins to reflect back to you the very things you are grateful for.

11

The Role of Detachment in Achieving Inner Peace

The Young Man:
(Sitting with his arms crossed, looking frustrated)
I feel like I'm constantly attached to the outcome of everything I do. Every little thing I try, I end up focusing so much on the result that I lose sight of the experience. How can I stop being so fixated on what I'll get from my efforts?

The Philosopher:
(With a knowing smile)
Ah, you are grappling with attachment. It is a common struggle. We often find ourselves so tied to the outcome that we forget to fully engage in the present moment. But here's the thing: attachment to results can cloud your judgment, breed anxiety, and create suffering. True peace comes when we learn to detach from the fruits of our labor, focusing instead on the act itself.

The Young Man:
(Looking confused)
Detach from the results? But aren't results what matter? How can I work towards something without caring about

what I'll get from it?

The Philosopher:

(Laughing softly)

You are not alone in that line of thinking. It's natural to want to succeed and be rewarded for your efforts. But let me share something Lord Krishna said in the Gita: *"You have the right to perform your prescribed duties, but you are not entitled to the fruits of your actions."* What Krishna is teaching us is that we must focus on the effort itself, without clinging to the outcomes. When you let go of the attachment to results, you free yourself from the anxiety and stress that come with them.

The Young Man:

(Pausing to think)

So, you're saying that I should care more about doing the work well, rather than stressing about the outcome? But what about my goals and ambitions?

The Philosopher:

(Nods thoughtfully)

Your goals are important, but how you pursue them is just as important. Krishna also said, *"Perform your actions with a detached mind, and let the results be the natural outcome of your efforts."* By detaching from the results, you allow yourself to give your best to the present moment, to the task at hand. When you are not bound by the fear of failure or the desire for success, you actually perform better, with more clarity and focus.

The Young Man:

(Nods slowly, starting to understand)

I see. So detachment doesn't mean giving up on my goals—it means freeing myself from the emotional rollercoaster of expecting certain outcomes?

The Philosopher:
(Smiling)
Exactly. Detachment allows you to remain at peace, no matter what happens. When you release the need for a specific outcome, you create space for more creativity and ease in your actions. You no longer carry the burden of constantly worrying about whether you will succeed or fail. This peace comes from within, and it is that peace that fuels sustained success.

The Young Man:
(Looking thoughtful)
But how do I practice detachment when it feels so difficult? I've been so used to tying my self-worth to my achievements.

The Philosopher:
(Sitting down beside him, with a calm demeanor)
The key to practicing detachment lies in finding joy in the process itself. Lord Krishna teaches us that *"One who is not attached to the fruits of their work, and who works as a matter of duty, is a true yogi."* It is not the rewards that define you, but the dedication with which you approach each task. By focusing on the process, not the outcome, you begin to find peace in simply doing. This is the path of inner fulfillment.

The Young Man:
(Slowly nodding, a sense of clarity in his eyes)
So, when I focus on the journey itself, I'm more likely to succeed because I'm not weighed down by my attachment to success or fear of failure. And I can still pursue my goals, but with less anxiety about the result.

The Philosopher:
(Smiling)
Exactly. When you approach life with detachment, you allow yourself to fully immerse in the present. You stop

worrying about things beyond your control and instead put your full energy into what is within your power to influence. Krishna reminds us that it's the dedication and the intention behind our actions that matter most, not the external rewards.

The Young Man:

(Looking up, feeling a sense of peace)

I think I understand now. I need to focus on the task at hand, without obsessing over the outcome. If I do that, I'll find peace, regardless of the results.

The Philosopher:

(With a deep, reassuring smile)

Yes. And remember, Krishna said *"When you perform your duty without attachment, you remain undisturbed by the results."* Detachment isn't about inaction—it's about moving through life with a calm heart, regardless of the external circumstances. It is the foundation of inner peace and true success.

The Young Man:

(With a calm smile)

Thank you. I feel lighter, like a weight has been lifted off my shoulders. I'm going to try practicing detachment and focus on doing my best without obsessing over the results.

The Philosopher:

(With a contented smile)

That's all you need to do. And in doing so, you'll find that life unfolds more peacefully, and you will achieve greater things than you ever thought possible.

12

The Power of Mind Control and Self-Discipline

The Young Man:
(Looking overwhelmed, distracted by his phone)
I've been struggling to stay focused lately. It's like my mind is always jumping from one thing to the next, and I can never seem to stay on task. How can I learn to control my mind?

The Philosopher:
(Laughing gently)
Ah, the restless mind. It is both our greatest strength and our greatest challenge. The mind can be like a wild horse, running in all directions. But the key to mastering it lies in discipline and self-control. As Lord Krishna said, *"The mind is restless, turbulent, and difficult to control, but it can be subdued by practice and detachment."*

The Young Man:
(Sitting up, intrigued)

So, you're saying that I can control my mind, but it takes practice? How do I even start?

The Philosopher:

(Nods thoughtfully)

Yes, practice and detachment are key. First, you must become aware of your mind's tendencies—where it wanders, what it clings to. Once you identify those distractions, you can begin to train your mind, just as you would train a horse. Krishna reminds us, "*A person who is self-controlled and disciplined in their actions achieves the highest goal.*"

The Young Man:

(Looking thoughtful)

That sounds like it requires a lot of work. How do I actually practice self-discipline when there's always something pulling me away?

The Philosopher:

(Smiling gently)

Discipline begins with small, consistent steps. Start by setting clear intentions for your day, and stick to them. Krishna teaches us that "*One who performs their duties with dedication, without any expectation of reward, is truly disciplined.*" It is not about grand gestures—it is about the small choices you make every day to focus your mind, to choose what truly matters, and to stay committed to your goals.

The Young Man:

(Nods slowly, starting to understand)

So, self-discipline isn't about forcing my mind to be perfect—it's about staying consistent and choosing focus, even when it's hard?

The Philosopher:

(With a serene smile)

Exactly. And remember, every time you choose to focus, every time you discipline your mind, you are strengthening your willpower. Krishna said, "*When the mind is controlled and the senses subdued, one can experience peace and spiritual fulfillment.*" With practice, you'll find that your mind becomes more steady, more aligned with your true purpose, and less distracted by external noise.

13

The Essence of Selflessness and Service

The Young Man:
(Sitting, looking pensive)
I've been thinking a lot lately about my ambitions and goals, but I'm also hearing a lot about the importance of helping others. I want to do well for myself, but I'm not sure how to balance that with being selfless. Does helping others take away from my own growth?

The Philosopher:
(Looking at him with compassion)
You are grappling with an important question, my young friend. It's a common dilemma—how can one be successful without losing sight of others? But let me share what Lord Krishna says about selflessness: *"A person who is not attached to the fruits of their actions, and who works with a spirit of service to others, is a true yogi."* When you serve others, you align yourself with a greater purpose, and in doing so, you don't lose anything—in fact, you gain far more than you can imagine.

The Young Man:
(Looking confused)
But if I'm always helping others, when will I have time to focus on myself and my goals? How can I help people and still grow?

The Philosopher:
(Smiling softly)
Ah, this is where the misconception lies. Service does not mean neglecting your own growth. It means expanding your vision beyond the self. Krishna teaches us that *"The highest form of devotion is to serve others without expecting anything in return."* When you dedicate yourself to the well-being of others, you tap into a deeper, more fulfilling source of growth. The more you give, the more you grow. Your growth is not diminished by your service—it is amplified.

The Young Man:
(Looking thoughtful)
I've always seen success as something I have to achieve on my own. How can helping others make me stronger or more successful?

The Philosopher:
(Pausing to reflect)
True success is not measured by what you achieve for yourself alone, but by how you contribute to the greater whole. When you serve others selflessly, you step outside your ego and align with a higher purpose. Krishna also says, *"One who is motivated by selfless love for others achieves the highest form of happiness."* The act of helping others frees you from selfish desires and brings you into harmony with the universe. This brings about an internal peace that no amount of personal success can provide.

The Young Man:
(Nods slowly)

So, you're saying that service isn't a sacrifice—it's actually a path to fulfillment? I always thought I had to choose between my own success and helping others, but now it seems like they can coexist.

The Philosopher:

(Smiling warmly)

Precisely. When you serve others, you are not giving up your own dreams—you are enriching them. Krishna teaches us that *"Actions performed with love and dedication to the welfare of others lead to spiritual fulfillment."* The more you focus on selfless service, the more you expand your heart and mind. You begin to see that your success is not isolated but interconnected with the well-being of others.

The Young Man:

(Looking inspired)

I think I understand now. Helping others doesn't take away from my own success. In fact, it enhances it. And I don't have to wait until I'm successful to start helping—I can do that right now.

The Philosopher:

(Nods)

Exactly. Service is not about waiting for the right moment. It is about choosing to help where you can, in any way you can. Krishna said, *"Perform your duty without attachment, and serve others without expectation."* The more you practice selflessness, the more you create space for grace and abundance in your life. And remember, true service comes from the heart—it is not about what you get, but about what you give.

The Young Man:

(Smiling, feeling lighter)

I think I'm starting to get it. The more I help others with no strings attached, the more peace and fulfillment I'll find.

And in doing so, I'll also find success that's deeper and more meaningful.

The Philosopher:

(With a knowing smile)

Exactly. And in that service, you will discover your true purpose and joy. When you serve with an open heart, you become a part of something much greater than yourself. This is the path of true fulfillment, and it is the key to lasting happiness.

14

The Strength of Acceptance and Surrender

The Young Man:
(Looking frustrated and tense)
I feel like I'm constantly trying to control everything in my life. I make plans, set goals, and try to control the outcomes, but life keeps throwing things my way that I didn't expect. How do I handle all these challenges? Why can't things just go the way I want?

The Philosopher:
(Laughing gently)
Ah, the desire to control. It is a powerful force within us, but it can also lead to great suffering. Life, my friend, is unpredictable. You cannot control everything, and trying to do so will only bring you frustration. But here's the wisdom Lord Krishna offers: *"Surrender to me completely, and I will take care of the rest."* When you let go of the need to control, you free yourself from unnecessary tension and allow life

to unfold as it is meant to.

The Young Man:

(Looking skeptical)

But how do I just surrender and let go? Doesn't that mean I'm giving up?

The Philosopher:

(With a calm and reassuring smile)

Surrender is not about giving up—it is about trusting the process. Krishna says, *"Give up all other forms of surrender and surrender to me alone, and I will liberate you from all sin."* Surrender means that you stop fighting life's flow. You acknowledge that some things are beyond your control, and instead of resisting them, you accept them as part of your journey. By doing so, you allow the divine to guide you.

The Young Man:

(Thinking carefully)

So, surrender isn't about doing nothing—it's about accepting what I can't change and trusting that there's a higher purpose at work?

The Philosopher:

(Smiling warmly)

Exactly. You still act, you still pursue your goals, but you do so with an understanding that the outcomes are not entirely in your hands. Krishna teaches us that *"When you surrender your actions to the divine, you perform them with peace and ease, without attachment to the results."* When you surrender, you release the burden of control and find peace in the uncertainty.

The Young Man:

(Looking more relaxed)

I think I understand now. Instead of fighting against what's happening, I need to trust that everything is happening for a reason and that the universe, or God, has a plan for me.

The Philosopher:

(Nods)

Yes. And remember, Krishna says, *"Those who surrender to me with faith and devotion will never be forsaken."* When you surrender, you open yourself up to divine guidance, peace, and strength. Trust that life is unfolding in its own time, and your role is to do your best with what you are given.

The Young Man:

(Smiling, feeling a sense of peace)

I feel a lot lighter now. I can still strive for my goals, but I don't have to control everything. I can trust the process and accept things as they come.

The Philosopher:

(With a deep, contented smile)

Yes, and in doing so, you will find that life becomes much more peaceful. Surrender is not weakness—it is the ultimate strength. When you trust in the flow of life, you allow it to support you in ways you cannot even imagine.

15

The Power of Persistence and Overcoming Setbacks

The Young Man:
(Sitting with frustration, tapping his fingers on the table)
I've been working so hard towards my goals, but it feels like every time I make progress, something happens to set me back. It's exhausting. How can I keep going when it feels like the world is against me?

The Philosopher:
(With a calm demeanor)
I understand your frustration. It's one of the most difficult experiences—the feeling that despite your best efforts, you keep facing obstacles. But let me share this: setbacks are a natural part of any journey. They don't define your path; your persistence does.

The Young Man:
(Looking doubtful)
It just feels like no matter how much I try, things never go

the way I plan. How do I keep pushing forward when it feels like everything is falling apart?

The Philosopher:

(Pausing thoughtfully)

It's in those very moments, when everything seems difficult, that your persistence matters most. Think of a tree. It grows through seasons of storms and harsh conditions, yet its roots remain grounded. Its branches stretch upward, even when the winds are fierce. Your persistence is your strength—it's what keeps you grounded and moving forward, even when the world tests you.

The Young Man:

(Starting to understand, but still unsure)

But what if I've been going for so long, and the results are still far away? How do I know if I'm on the right track?

The Philosopher:

(Smiling gently)

You won't always know immediately if you're on the right track, and that uncertainty can be uncomfortable. But what's important is that you continue. You've already taken the first step by setting out. Now, every setback is a chance to learn, refine, and adapt. Every obstacle is an opportunity for growth. It's not about how many times you fall, but about how many times you get back up.

The Young Man:

(Nods slowly)

So, it's not about perfection—it's about showing up and continuing, even when things don't go as planned?

The Philosopher:

(With a knowing smile)

Exactly. True success isn't about avoiding failure; it's about learning from it. Every challenge you face is a lesson in resilience. The most successful people didn't achieve their goals without facing hardship. They simply persisted through it. It's your ability to keep moving forward that defines your success, not the smoothness of the path.

The Young Man:

(Leaning in, more focused)

That makes sense. But how do I stay motivated when everything seems to be going wrong?

The Philosopher:

(Leaning back, relaxed)

Motivation can be fleeting, especially when things are difficult. That's where discipline comes in. Discipline is the force that keeps you going when motivation wanes. It's the commitment to your long-term vision, regardless of the immediate setbacks. Setbacks will test your resolve, but your discipline will carry you through. It's like the habit of taking one step at a time, even when the destination seems far off.

The Young Man:

(Reflecting)

So, the key isn't to wait for things to get easier or for motivation to kick in. It's about building the discipline to keep going, no matter the circumstances.

The Philosopher:

(With a soft smile)

Exactly. The world will always present challenges, but how you respond to them is what shapes your journey. By maintaining your persistence and adapting your approach, you'll grow stronger with each setback. Success isn't just about reaching a destination—it's about the person you become along the way.

The Young Man:

(Smiling, a sense of resolve in his eyes)

I see now. It's not about avoiding obstacles; it's about facing them and continuing forward. The challenges are part of the process, and I can use them to build my strength.

The Philosopher:

(Nods approvingly)

Well said. The greatest achievements often come after the toughest trials. So long as you keep moving, keep learning, and stay true to your purpose, success will follow. Remember, persistence isn't about speed—it's about endurance

16

Finding Balance Between Ambition and Contentment

The Young Man:
(Sitting thoughtfully, looking a bit restless)
I've been chasing success for so long, but lately, I've been feeling like something's missing. I want to achieve more, but I also want to feel content with where I am now. How do I balance the drive for success with appreciating what I already have?

The Philosopher:
(Pausing to reflect)
It's a great question. Many people find themselves stuck in the same dilemma—how to push forward without feeling that they're constantly chasing something outside of themselves. The answer lies in understanding that ambition and contentment don't have to be opposites. They can coexist, and in fact, they support each other.

The Young Man:
(Looking confused)
How can I be content with where I am while still pushing for more? Isn't wanting more the opposite of being satisfied with what I already have?

The Philosopher:
(Smiling)
It's about perspective. Contentment doesn't mean complacency—it means appreciating what you have at the moment while still striving for growth. Think of it like planting a tree. You care for it, nurture it, and watch it grow. You're content with the tree as it is right now, but you still desire it to reach its fullest potential. Similarly, you can be content with your present self, while also pursuing new goals to become the best version of yourself.

The Young Man:
(Nods slowly)
So, it's not about being passive or settling for less—it's about appreciating the process of growth and being grateful for what you have while working toward more.

The Philosopher:
(With a warm smile)
Exactly. The key is gratitude. When you focus on what you have now and are thankful for it, you create a sense of fulfillment that comes from within. This fulfillment then fuels your ambition. You don't chase success out of lack—you chase it because it's a natural extension of who you are becoming. It's not about what you don't have—it's about what you can create from what you already have.

The Young Man:
(Smiling, starting to see the balance)
I think I get it now. It's about enjoying the journey and finding fulfillment in the present, even as I continue to

grow. Ambition is important, but it shouldn't make me lose sight of what I already have.

The Philosopher:

(With a gentle nod)

Exactly. Contentment is not the absence of ambition, but the recognition that you are enough, right here, right now. When you combine that peace with your ambition, you become unstoppable. Success will come, not as a result of constant striving, but from a place of deep fulfillment and clarity.

Conclusion

The Path Forward

The Philosopher (The Philosopher):
(Leaning forward with a look of wisdom)
You've asked many thoughtful questions, and I can see that you are beginning to understand a deeper way of living—one that values persistence, selflessness, and balance. Life will always present challenges, and while the journey is rarely easy, it's in the way we approach these challenges that we find our true strength. Whether it's embracing setbacks as opportunities for growth, serving others without expecting anything in return, or balancing ambition with contentment, the path forward is shaped not by external circumstances but by your inner resolve.

The Young Man (The Young Man):
(Sitting with a sense of calm, reflecting)
I feel like I have a clearer vision now. It's not about avoiding the struggles or trying to control everything. It's about how I respond to them. I can continue working hard, but without losing sight of the present moment or the bigger picture. My goals can be meaningful without making me feel empty if I keep my focus on growth, gratitude, and helping others along the way.

The Philosopher:
(Smiling warmly)
Exactly. Life's true beauty comes from the journey, not just the destination. As you continue to pursue your goals, remember to embrace each step along the way. Stay grounded in your purpose, be open to the lessons each day brings, and always keep a sense of gratitude for what you have and who you are becoming. In this balance, you will

find a fulfillment that transcends mere success.

The Young Man:

(Nods with determination)

Thank you for guiding me through this. I now see that I can pursue my ambitions with a sense of peace and balance, not just for myself, but for others too. I feel ready to face whatever comes next.

The Philosopher:

(With a deep, knowing smile)

And that is the true essence of a fulfilling life—walking with purpose, embracing challenges, and growing not only for yourself but for the greater good of those around you. Remember, the journey never truly ends, and with each step, you evolve into the best version of yourself. Trust the process, stay committed, and know that you are always exactly where you need to be.

Closing Statement

As you turn the final pages of this book, know that your journey has just begun. The Journey to the Self is not meant to end here. The lessons, insights, and reflections shared within these pages are stepping stones on the path to the person you are destined to become.

This book has been a companion, but the real work lies within you. It is in your actions, your choices, and your commitment to continue growing, questioning, and evolving. As you move forward, remember that each day offers an opportunity for self-discovery, for change, and for transformation. The path will not always be easy, but it will always be yours to walk.

What you have learned here is not just theory—it is a living practice. It is in how you show up each day, in how you speak to yourself and others, and in how you choose to create a life of meaning and purpose. Embrace the power of awareness, discipline, and inner strength. Lead with authenticity, and leave a legacy that reflects the truest version of who you are.

The journey never truly ends, for there is always more to discover within yourself. So, take what you've learned, carry it with you, and continue to move forward. Be the change you seek, and inspire those around you to do the same. The world needs the unique gift that only you can offer.

Thank you for trusting this book to be a part of your journey. I wish you peace, purpose, and the courage to walk the path toward your true self.

With all my heart,
Raghu. Jupudi

www.ingramcontent.com/pod-product-compliance
Lightning Source LLC
Chambersburg PA
CBHW051607130726
48053CB00038B/164

* 9 7 9 8 8 9 9 0 6 2 1 6 2 *